First Facts™

The Senses

Touching

by Rebecca Olien

Consultant:
Eric H. Chudler, PhD, Research Associate Professor
Department of Anesthesiology, University of Washington
Seattle, Washington

Capstone *press*
Mankato, Minnesota

First Facts is published by Capstone Press,
151 Good Counsel Drive, P.O. Box 669, Mankato, Minnesota 56002.
www.capstonepress.com

Library of Congress Cataloging-in-Publication Data
Olien, Rebecca.
    Touching / by Rebecca Olien.
    p. cm. —(First facts. The senses)
    Summary: "Explains the sense of touch and how the skin works as a sense organ"—Provided
by publisher.
    Includes bibliographical references and index.
    ISBN 0-7368-4305-1 (hardcover)
    1. Touch—Juvenile literature. I. Title. II. Series.
QP451.O44 2006
612.8'8—dc22   2004027216

Editorial Credits
Wendy Dieker, editor; Juliette Peters, designer; Kelly Garvin, photo researcher/photo editor

Photo Credits
Capstone Press/Jim Foell, 16–17; Karon Dubke, cover, 10, 12, 13, 14–15, 21
Corbis, Pete Saloutos, 19; RF, 10 (background); Ted Horowitz, 1, 11
Getty Images Inc./Burke/Triolo Productions, 5; Gary Braasch, 8–9
Photo Researchers/Science Photo Library/Pascal Goetgheluck, 20

1 2 3 4 5 6 10 09 08 07 06 05

Table of Contents

The Sense of Touch

Our senses help us discover the world around us. We use five senses to hear, see, smell, taste, and touch. We use skin to touch. The skin has **sensors** that help us feel if things are hot, cold, rough, or smooth.

Fun Fact!

An adult's skin covers as much space as 30 sheets of notebook paper.

The Skin

The skin has two layers. The outer layer is the **epidermis**. The inner layer of skin is the **dermis**.

The dermis holds touch sensors. Different sensors detect different things. Each sensor sends messages to the brain through the **nerves**. The brain tells us what we feel.

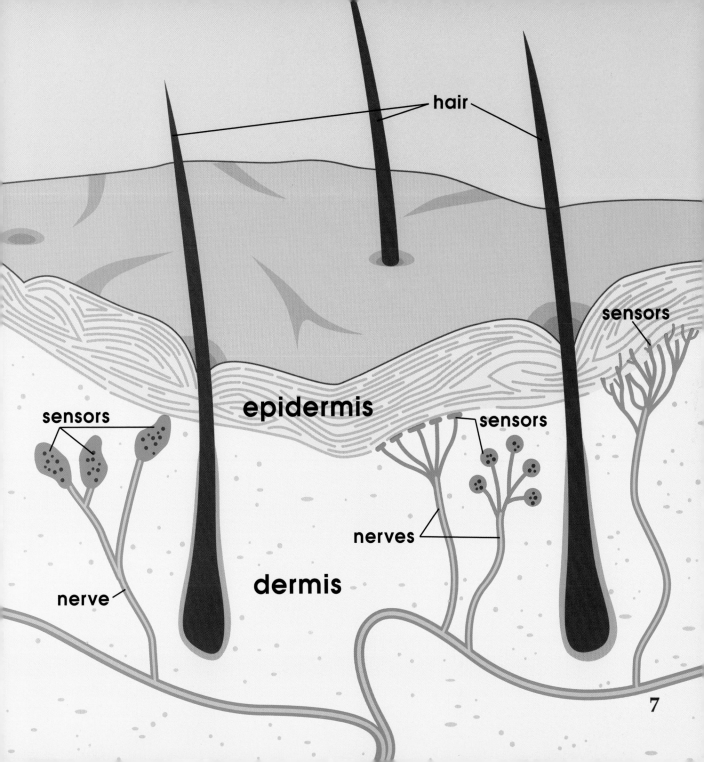

Touch Sensors

Every part of the skin has touch sensors. Some sensors help you feel different **textures**. You can feel the difference between a rough tree trunk and a smooth leaf.

! Fun Fact!
Messages travel from a touch sensor to the brain in less than one second.

9

More Touch Sensors

The skin also has sensors to help you feel **temperature**. Some sensors can help you feel the coldness of a snowball. Other sensors help you feel heat.

Your skin has many sensors for pain. Pain is an alarm. It tells you something is wrong. Pain tells you to stop doing what hurts.

Messages from Sensors

Some sensors send messages for a short time. At first, a swimming pool feels cold. Then sensors stop sending messages. The water no longer feels cold.

Pain sensors keep sending messages
to the brain. A stone in your shoe
keeps hurting your foot until you take
it out.

Taking Care of Skin

Skin needs care to stay healthy. Washing your hands and body cleans off dirt and germs. Cuts and scrapes heal better with cleaning and bandages. Lotion helps skin stay soft.

Fun Fact!

How long should you wash your hands? Wash long enough to sing the "Happy Birthday" song.

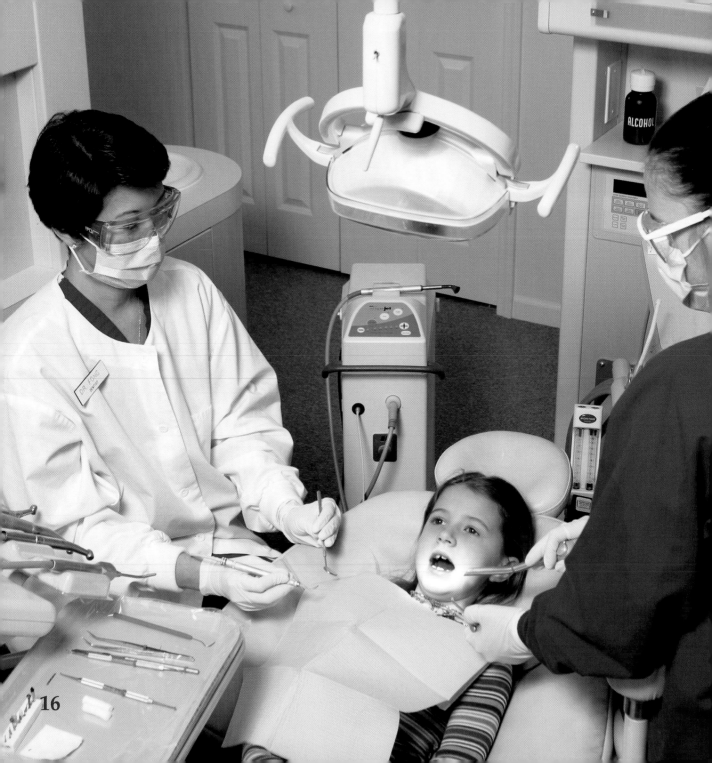

Loss of Feeling

Some drugs keep nerves from sending messages to the brain. A dentist gives a shot to numb the mouth. Then the dentist can do work that would be painful without the drugs.

Cats Use Touch

Animals have senses too. Cats' **whiskers** have touch sensors. In the dark, cats move their whiskers forward to search in front of themselves. Whiskers rub against objects. Their whiskers help cats avoid bumping into things.

Fun Fact!
Cats also have whiskers on their eyebrows, their chins, and the backs of their front legs.

Scientists have invented machine hands with sensors that can feel objects. These hands are used on robots. Robots work better with sensors. They can pick up dangerous objects, like bombs. People can stay safe when robots do dangerous jobs.

Hands On: Glove Game

Gloves protect our hands but also make feeling more difficult. Play this game with a friend or on your own.

What You Need

paper bag
3 or more objects with
    different textures and shapes
garden glove
rubber glove

What You Do

1. Place all the different objects in the bag.
2. While wearing a garden glove, reach into the bag and feel an object. Guess what it is. Then pull it out to see if you are right. Feel each object in the bag.
3. Place the objects back into the bag. Try again while wearing the rubber glove.
4. Finally, feel the objects without wearing a glove.

    Which glove made feeling the objects the most difficult? Could you guess what the objects were while wearing the gloves?

Glossary

dermis (DUR-mis)—the layer of skin under the epidermis

epidermis (ep-ih-DUR-mis)—the outer layer of skin; the epidermis is the layer of skin we see.

nerve (NURV)—a thin fiber that carries messages between the brain and other parts of the body

sensor (SEN-sur)—a body part that sends messages to the nerves

temperature (TEM-pur-uh-chur)—how hot or cold something is

texture (TEKS-chur)—the roughness or smoothness of something

whisker (WISS-kur)—a long stiff hair growing on the face and bodies of some animals

Read More

Cobb, Vicki. *Feeling Your Way: Discover Your Sense of Touch.* Brookfield, Conn.: Millbrook Press, 2001.

Levine, Shar, and Leslie Johnstone. *Super Senses.* First Science Experiments. New York: Sterling, 2003.

Murphy, Patricia J. *Touch.* A True Book. New York: Children's Press, 2003.

Internet Sites

FactHound offers a safe, fun way to find Internet sites related to this book. All of the sites on FactHound have been researched by our staff.

Here's how:
1. Visit *www.facthound.com*
2. Type in this special code **0736843051** for age-appropriate sites. Or enter a search word related to this book for a more general search.
3. Click on the **Fetch It** button.

FactHound will fetch the best sites for you!

Index